Metaphors and Praises

~Poetic JB~

Sources of scriptures in this book are from:

Editor: Stephen Smith.

Publication date: Oct 20, 2021.

Publisher: OpenBible.info.

https://www.openbible.info/topics/king_james_bible

Giving Honor

First and foremost, I thanked the Most High, our amazing

Heavenly Father for the many blessings upon my life. I would

be nothing without His presence and I will praise His name,

all the days of my life!

Thank you, Father!

Sincerely,

~Your Poetic Daughter~

Welcome God's Children

Enjoy this book of praises

Worship poetry

Good Morning

Grasping that first breath of fresh air,

when your eyelids slowly open

Looking around without a fear,

that things are still in tact

You move the limbs you fell asleep with,

stretching them awake

Glancing out your window,

taking time out to listen to nature

Realizing how beautiful,

the sun rays, light up everything

Thinking to yourself,

"God has done this all for me"

that you are bless

Good Morning

Waking up in the mornings and giving thanks to my

Father, for restoring me, everyday. Made me see the vessel

He wants me to be and the protection that keeps me from

dangers others have tried against me. You see...the enemy

wants me sad and lonely because he sees me happy, filled

with joy, but like in Ephesians, I stay armed up and at the

ready. Steady, with our Father on my side, I can defeat

anything because He strengthens me.

Yah (God) Bless You & Yah (God) Bless Me...

Have a Great Day!

Put on the full armor of Elohiym (God), so that you can

take your stand against the devil's schemes.

Ephesians 6:11

Those Hymns

Don't dim down my smile,

because you don't understand my praise

Some say words are just words

But maybe,

they've never had to speak life into their day

I'm a firm believer that,

when praises go up

blessings are sure enough,

to come down

Singing through the storm,

helps the sun shine through those broken clouds

Sending hope to areas of grey,

that only God can take away

So excuse yourself

while I give my life, life

through my voice

through my poetry

through my song

Planting seeds of positivity,

infused water with encouraging vitamins

To quench my thirsty roots

I have chosen,

to speak the right recipe

into my light

Despite the naysayers,

of my praise

I never would have made it!

Never would have made it,

through my darkened nights,

without sowing all I had at that moment & time,

to the Most High

Pockets filled with emptiness,

inhaling sin

I gave what only,

I had deep within

My song

My praise

My voice

Those hymns

Your praises are not in vain...

Someone once said, "Those hymns won't save a dang thing!" I couldn't digest that because I know different. I sang praises through every bad situation I ever had and still do. I sing praises, when I feel good, when I feel down, and when I just want to render my voice to tell our Gracious Father, Thank you. So keep praising and don't let anyone ever tell you that your praises don't mean anything.

Praise On!

Tell Me

Tell me again, why you can speak?

Woke up this morning, watched the sun peak

over the horizon, you were smiling...not crying

Tell me again, why you can't pray?

Your kids are awoke, came into your room,

Spoke, kissed you, said, "They are on their way"

Tell me again, why you can't share?

Your burdens are not for you to bear

He's always there to uplift you

Tell me again, why you can't praise?

He gave you the breath of life

A book of instructions and a will to fight

Tell me again, why you can't?

By him therefore let us offer the sacrifice of praise to Elohiym

(God) continually, that is, the fruit of our lips giving thanks to

his name. But to do good and to communicate forget not: for

with such sacrifices Elohiym (God) is well pleased.

Hebrews 13:15-16

Replenishing

Don't shower me with money

Shower me with God's green trees

give me oxygen to breathe

Forget the gold and diamonds

Show me the flower gardens

of Mother Nature's soil

Refill my energy, Nourish my soul

Replenish me

I find myself indulging in God's creation. In every breath of air to every grain of soil that was made for us. I find my peace within His creation walking around barefoot with the sun beaming upon me. Praying and Praising in His glory, He, restores me.

My First Love

Falling in Love with my first Love

Who would have thought,

that's all I've ever needed?

Tired of doing things my way

My other life had to be deleted

Forgive me for the sins, I've completed

I love you, I'm sorry that I've cheated

I'm ready to be fully committed to you

To your will, I chose to do

Living this life without you, I refuse

Falling in Love with my first Love

Father, that's you!

I was so busy loving different object and people, I lost handle of my first love. The one who gave me life, a purpose, and a voice, how could I have been so blinded? The creator of all creation, my first love!

Just Me

I'm here to reclaim all of my many mansions

From the tip of many pushing pens

To the bottom of the last lines,

where words become squished in

Gonna' sustain it, maintain it

Poetry is where my ultimate aim is

God is my number one go to

Faith is my super power,

where it all comes through

I can do anything I bring my mind too

Believing in my dreams

Coming out of the hell hole

Retrieving my destiny

Dreams

I got tired of my dreams

leaning on me while I slept

Woke up head hurting

thinking I wasn't the best

My fear had the most of me

Kept hold of me

Controlling me

While I, kept myself bound

Now I live my dreams

Fears, nowhere to be found

My dreams now watch me in my sleep

I get rest at night

the taste of success is so sweet

If Yah (God) can do it for me

Best believe

He'll do it for you

Walk in your faith

Put down your doubtful issues

Let it do, what HE do

For the Gentiles seek after all these things, and your

heavenly Father knows that you need them all. But seek first

the kingdom of Elohiym (God) and his righteousness, and all

these things will be added to you.

Therefore do not be anxious about tomorrow, for tomorrow

will be anxious for itself. Sufficient for the day is its own

trouble.

Matthew 6:32-34

Vent It Out

I had a major step back, back in the day, because I made my decisions, didn't follow God's ways, had to buckle down, change for the better, now my faith is larger than my cheddar. The vision I have for my life is bigger than this World, I kept hush to keep up the push, dug down deep, kept my eye on the prize, soon I'll be there in no time, but before I get off here there's something on my mind...

You have to be determined for what you want, If not, you're going be like everybody else, mind blank, no escape, sitting up on the block, over using the words such as, "I cannot," married to fear, side piece is doubt, no confidence in your walk, stalked by intimidation, limiting your own expectations, even your unbelief has disbelief, wanting to be a Chief yet, not spiritually grounded, hating on others success, cause your lack of knowledge is rounded, motivationally dumbfounded, depending on others to carry your dreams, not realizing you're

owned, while you love on your bitterness that trapped you in

the first place, it is you that has to step out on faith, get out

your comfy uncomfortable place, take a stand in your life

before you get replaced, don't let excuses be your escape, no

one said it would be easy, there's going to be some tears, more

than a few, just lift your head to the sky, put in the work, I

promise you, everything will do what it do, if you put God

first!

My self-reflection is necessary. Speaking to my inner

spirit is necessary. Accountability for my choices is necessary.

I had to point the finger at myself and tell myself to get it

together. No one could make me put God first; I had to want

Him first!

Control Thyself

Trust me, when I say

I can understand your heartaches

Been down a road of much pain

lost, unfound, feeling unloved

This world don't hand you a perfect life

In Fact...

It's filled with down falls, depression,

and very bad advice

Had to go into this cold world

as a young parent

making plan B & C, all the way to Z

this place wasn't made to gracefully get by

I had rough obstacles

with many cliffs to climb

Days filled with tunnel vision

black outs, not knowing which way to go

wanting to go right

Yet, left seems so right

making decisions that left me without a home

Found myself, a Queen crying on her throne

feeling as if, I couldn't do anything right

crying all day, bawling at night

Anxiety got the best of me

let worry caress me

My fears controlled the rest of me

things couldn't change, stressed me

Nothing that I did was pleasing

relationship break-ups became easy

heartaches became numb

Times I sat there looking dumb

staring into outer space

wishing death could take my place

wanting the world to blow up

so I wouldn't have to face it alone

Until I...realized It was up to me, to change it

Looking in my mirror, it was me

A reflection of my problems

   "It's my world, they're just living in it"

my brother's voice, I pondered

Had to stop making excuses for myself

start playing the hand that I dealt

Facing reality became easier

day by day, I felt less colder

My walk by faith got bolder

started speaking greatness over my life

Positive vibes right out my mouth

had to give my life back to my maker

Thank God, for mercy and a savior

Nothing that I have came easy

The will to not give up

was stronger than my will to eat

Your girl had hit rock bottom

Started making right decision got rid of "my insanity"

God started leaving blessings at my feet

not without a soulful lesson though

God promised to never let me go

The best lesson was myself

taking responsibility for me, no one else

I swam through the struggle

Danced in the rain

I thank God daily

that I,

am not the same

Overcome

Swallowed by fear,

    drowning in tears

Chugging your sorrows,

    with wounds of tomorrow

Coming down on yourself,

    feeling sorry for yourself

Letting the enemy know,

    you're defeated

Disrespected by the unworthy,

    not standing your ground

Your pride is showing through

    your frown?

Stop...

    take a deep breath

Now listen...

Get up out that festering wound,

you created

Take back the power God gave to you,

   for after all, you're His creation

Stand your ground,

   shine in His grace

Respect yourself,

   watch those who broke you, get replaced

Overcome the obstacles,

   that seem impossible

Drink your armor,

   swallow that fear

Start swimming in faith,

   pathways He'll clear

Put the "S" on your chest,

   Show the World you're are Victorious

Be like Byrd the Overcomer, don't stress

God's got it

a seed of prayer

a plea of faith

in no time

You'll be an Overcomer in a brand new place

Nay, in all these things we are more than conquerors through him that loved us. For I am persuaded, that neither death, nor life, nor angels, nor principalities, nor powers, nor things present, nor things to come, Nor height, nor depth, nor any other creature, shall be able to separate us from the love of Elohiym, which is in Mashiach Yahusha our Adonai.

Romans 8:37-39.

Let's Pause: *Words to Know*

I like using Hebrew names, yet, I would like everyone to understand.

Yah = God

Elohiym = Supreme God, Creator of Heaven and Earth.

Mashiach = Anointed Messiah, Christ

Yahusha = Son of God, Jesus

Adonai = Master, Lord

Let us continue...

Forgive Them

I need you

I need you

to wrap

your strong arms

Around you

Now squeeze until you feel

your heartbeat (feel it?)

Now close your eyes

Picture everything that you ever been through

And Say,

I...forgive you

You, meaning you

You're not the reason

they

didn't love you

You are not the reason

they raised their fist to you

You are not the reason

for the hate

Or the mistreatment

Forgive yourself for not thinking of yourself,

      deserving more

Forgive yourself for

putting up with them

Most importantly

Forgive yourself for not

forgiving them

Deep down inside

One thought of them

Makes you cringe

The hurt they caused

battered feeling and

loneliness within

Release the burden

feel the peace

Find what makes you happy

And just live again

Live a life you always dreamed of

Knowing that it isn't the end

That there will be love again

Not everyone is him or her

Not everyone has come to harm you

Not everyone is them

Now

I need you to wrap your arms around you

And say,

"I love you

even though I've made mistakes

To harm you

I forgive you

But because I deserve my peace,

I forgive them."

     Forgiving others was one obstacle I had to face. When I found that easy to do, I still felt a bit of emptiness. This too a lot of self reflection and no matter how I wanted to turn, it was always looking in the mirror. It was me that I needed to forgive. That's the hardest pill to swallow. I broke myself and allowed myself to get hurt because I wasn't on my right path. Self forgiveness was a must for me. After all, the word says to forgive, so why not with the man in the mirror first.

For if you forgive others their trespasses, your heavenly Father will also forgive you, but if you do not forgive others their trespasses, neither will your Father forgive your trespasses.

Matthew 6:14-15

Life Anchor

If I can't be honest with you,

then who?

Living blinded

by the problem at hand

No man, wanting to love,

could ever understand

So I stay drifting on my sailboat

with just enough wind,

not to reach shore

Call it my safe haven,

if you must

Letting the waves be my comfort

As they seem to be like my emotions

Calm, smooth,

choppy, and rough

I'll let the wind comfort my heart

The rain, quench my thirst

I'll stay afloat until

God gives me

My life anchor

Be careful choosing the anchor that holds you down to your foundation, some may anchor you in the middle of a storm.

~P.JB~

Until my Soul Cried

I am,

    the love,

        that I seek

I am enough for others

      especially for me

Not to take away from the Most High

      without him

My wings would have never opened

      to soar high

I never knew

    A love like this...

           Until my soul cried

There was no happiness

      that could ever compare

Left me inside a state

      of a great vibe

I am,

    the joy,

        that I desired

The peace

        I desperately yearned for

For years

        never thought

My soul could cry

        until I broke up with the doubt in me

Left fear sitting on a bench that I,

        was once glued too

Searching for me

        but I, was long gone away

Embracing myself down to the

        ugliest energy, every single day

Putting my Faith in the Father

        was the best thing that could happen to me

Separation of my house and the enemy

        took me to unbelievable, beautiful peaks

Never turning back to those darkened

        confused streets, I wanted more

My tongue was dabbed with

        spiritual freedom

My mind swallows up knowledge

        so I can help feed His people

I never knew completion

        like this...

           Until my soul cried

Started off, lost and cold

        not knowing which way to go

Young, dumb, full of my selfish ego

        to grown to listen to wisdom from the old

I had to swallow my pride

        let go, let God, & stride down a narrow line

I was taken above my expectation

      filled with joy, I didn't know existed

This is where I found out

      My soul could cry

Not because I'm trampled down & battered

      not from brokenness, hurt, or pain

      not due to a man who wants to take my hand &

      love me in all the right ways

But

Because my soul feels complete

    I'm in love with His son

    loneliness doesn't exist when I am

   feeling content reading about the Most High above

I feel loved, in many ways, not just one

I am a child in His Kingdom

      you can believe what you want

I never knew my soul could cry

Until

I learned to love the Yah/God in me

The God in me...

So here I am in my life, thinking all tears were caused by pain and tribulations. I failed to realize that I was made in His image and our Father gave the tools that we need in this realm. I underestimated that verse and didn't study like I should have, but when I really applied that to my life, things started to fall into place and my faith was elevated. I understood that he had already anchored me down to him, I was choosing to detach from his foundation, putting other "gods" before him. I surrendered and my soul cried out for joy. I am His Child and belong to His Kingdom! That's exciting!

So Elohiym created man in his own image, in the image of Elohiym he created him; male and female he created them.

Genesis 1:27

Lost Soul

Perhaps you lost yourself trying to be an image that you were never made to be.

Lost in a land where you can't find the real voice that comes from deep within, saying, "me."

You wore around images that only portrayed you as others, covering what God created you to be.

Your mind, wrapped around an object you have seen fitting, yet, you don't know this person that you call, "me."

Perhaps you're Jordan, Gucci, or an image that you can't afford?

Stressing out to fit in a World, you were never built for!

Wanting something greater by painting yourself with labels that are less than the royalty flowing through your toes
You'd fake your life just to please eyes whom stab you deliberately in the back

Perhaps you've been searching for you in all these items, confused on what to be or who to be

You've lost yourself so much that you can't even say, "Me" with meaning.

As the Rain Drops

As the rain drops

into my blessed soul

Heart still yelling,

let it go, let it go

Tired of unnecessary

Hurt and pain

Wondering where ya been?

Who ya doing?

Will I ever amount the same?

Driving me insane

As the rain drops,

into my blessed soul

Heart still yelling

let it go, let it go

Giving...to only

Have nothing left for me

Struggling to make ends meet

Yet, gracious enough

to still fill your cup

While mine

remains empty

As the rain drops,

into my blessed soul

Heart still yelling

let it go, let it go

Frustrated from drama

Friends of fakeness

made of eraser crumbles

that come together

Little by little

Ridding my hard working

Existence

As the rain drops,

into my blessed soul

Heart still yelling

let it go, let it go

My urge to give up

Attacks at my weakest

Leaving me feeling ashamed

Not knowing how

To control the

these negative thoughts

to blow my brain

Continuing to rot

in this sick body of mine

As the rain drops,

into my blessed soul

Heart still yelling

let it go, let it go

If I can love them

more than I love me...

If I can help them

more than I can help myself...

If I can give them loyalty

more than I give my health...

If I can't give up on me

more than it's telling me...

Let it go, Let it go

Heart still yelling

Into my blessed soul

As the rain drops

LET GO & LET GOD!

I Wanted

I wanted that feel good life, the one where you smile

Take advice, roll the dice to your next destination

Take you to new heights, making fancy reservations

Seeing every piece of God's beautiful creations

Rain, sleet, or snow, pack the bags

We end up on the hot shores or up the cold mountain peaks

I wanted

to end up where my mouth speaks

life lives in the walls of my cheeks

with no fear, no doubt

Just prayer, add faith, hard work and praise it out

Knowing my bad days, won't outweigh my good

As I am grounded in He, He gives me life

a breath of grace air, fresher than my first breath

I wanted

to be free from hurt, stress, and depression

For people to see a light in me

A light that only God could bless

that ray of hope on the worse day

That, "I can do if she can" life

to be used for His purpose

A bigger vessel than I seen for my life

I wanted

to be His, solely for His Kingdom

Where I know I'd be safe & have salvation

My safe haven, where I'm caught when I fall

Loved, when I'm alone

Given rest, when I'm out of energy

That fire for His glory

Show His greatness through my story

Every testimony told, was God showing out for me

ALL Praises to Him

I wanted

so I prayed...

Had faith & I got it

I know that He loves me, Glory!

But seek first the kingdom of Elohiym and his righteousness,

and all these things will be added to you.

Matthew 6:33

Seek the Kingdom?

Do we really know what this verse means as believers? I mean, I thought I did. I can only speak for myself on this. I thought if I go to church and participate then that was seeking the Kingdom. BOYYYY, was I wrong! Spiritual growth was needed. I began to pray, read, and study to find myself approved all the time, as the Word states, ya know? (1 Timothy 2:15) This walk activated my Faith even more so, and I wanted to be obedient to His word. I wanted truth, clarity, understanding and His wisdom and knowledge.

Of course, I am still growing, but I've seen my words and prayers come to life and I can only thank our Father for His helping hands. So yea, seek the Kingdom for yourself and watch Yah work in your life.

Breathe

((Breathe)) Woosah

A term used to blow off steam when you really want to be

mean, Using angry words that will break a person's ego, but

naw, you just let it go

((Breathe))) Woosahhhhh

As if that little word of air can compare to your throbbing

heart rate, making your tummy ache because the stress is too

much to digest, yet somehow you haven't exploded into

particles within their membrane

((Breathe)) Woooosahhhh

Releasing positive hot air into your element, not causing a

scene, you zip it. Keeping the peace chanting prayers under

your breath, hoping God can do the rest, catch you before you.

((Breathe)) Wooosahhhh

Catch you before you go in on what you feel, not caring if your

tongue could kill, in which your mind has done over & over

again, forgive me for my sins, I promise my thoughts are only

within

((Breathe)) Wooosahhh

Until you feel better or pass out because this breathing mess

is making you light headed, calming down takes energy, not

to give them your negativity, in which you're biting your

tongue on a daily

So you breathe in and out

Woosah here, Woosah there

Getting burnt out!

So the floor becomes the safe haven,keeping you grounded,

you start to praying, closing your eyes, zoning out to the

sound of your heart beat, the little voice in your head asking God to help you through this trying time, having faith that He'll pull you through like the times before, reminding you that there's a blessing in stored, just keep praising your way through, the light will shine again, you'll get through this again, it's only for a season to prepare you for what's to come, lessons learned, you have still Won. Yah will never leave you or forsake you, it's already done!

((Breathe)) ((Breathe)) ((Breathe))

HalleluYah! I'm done.

Know this, my beloved brothers: let every person be quick to hear, slow to speak, slow to anger; for the anger of man does not produce the righteousness of Elohiym.
James 1:19-20

Every Tear Dropped

Every tear dropped
     becomes my strength
Somehow, survival skills
     are applied
I'm choked up with faith
     rather than,
Smoke that fades
     leaving me worse,
Than how I felt
     "a strong state of mind of being content"
With my Father holding
     my fragile soul
He promised
     to never forsake me
Or to leave me alone

          Everyone; once upon a time
               felt the darkness appear
          Some ran; out of fear
               still lost today
          Others reached out

gained a magnitude of faith

Allowed God to be the light
    to light their broken pathways
Some put up a fight
    they're still swinging till this day
Not understanding
    their rest, is in the best
The Most High Yah, don't play

    Yah is my peace
        in the midst of any storm
    Keeps me grounded
        when I feel torn
    Many wonder,
        how I do what I do
    My smile keeps the enemy
        confused
    God will always get the glory
        that's the definition of my story
    Every tear dropped
        praises consumed my thoughts
    My tongue speaks life

I'm addicted to faith

Working with God's grace

    rather lost in His Kingdom

Than dancing on a fiery lake, but Yah

When my tears fell, I used to think it was a sign of weakness. I never wanted to cry. I wanted to be strong and hold them in and be tough. Then I realized that it felt good to get them out. Everyone has their opinion about crying. Well mine...gave me strength. My tears usually came from being hurt. I was able to reflect back on the times when I was crying and didn't think I would ever get out of that feeling of disappointment. Then I look at how I can praise my way through these times and I no longer feel stuck. I learned from my tears and faith that no matter how bad or hard it seems, our Father had everything already worked out. Each time, my faith grew. Each time, my strength grew. Each time, God made a way.

Learn how to praise your way through your tears.

This Bible

Dedicated to my Spiritual Father, Apostle Timothy Shockley, Elder Hadar. Thank you for the bible...

This Bible that I hold
Knows more of my Soul
Then I'll ever know

It's heard and understood
My yells and pleads
From every ripped page
To the edges creased
It holds a part of me
That you'll never meet

The pages and creases
Have tasted my tears
When I was in despair
Helped me face my fears
When felt I couldn't

My pillow
For those nights
When I couldn't find peace
My headrest
When I was weak

Some lines know
My deepest weeps
While others...laughter
After reading the truth it speaks
All those highlighted and pen marked pages

Know my war
They've seen my scars
For my story it's their to tell

It has been my best friend
When I felt no one cared
My advisor
When I was confused
My comfort
When I've been scared

Everyone talks about God
But without his word...
How far would you have gone?

My bible
My atlas to life
My directions in my lessons
The book of the best advice

These pages
Have felt my heart beat
Through my fingertips

The sweat on my forehead
From those rough days
When I couldn't
Seem to ease the pain

It's heard my deepest prayers
My wonders and worries
My questions of clarity
The who's, what's, when's, where's, and how's
And of course

Sometimes why's
From my curious mind
It carries my pathway
Closer to God
And knows what
Obstacles I walk on

It knows the vibe I give
Off the first initial grab
How I'm feeling
Just by how I'm flipping the pages
It knows more about my heart
Then I know of myself

For I was created
By its creator
To create me

((I'll say that again))

For I was created
By its creator
To create me

Like me
It's dingy, used up
Marked, torn, and worn
But we still carry
A strong purpose

For our work
Is not done

You can tell a lot about someone's prayer life by the looks of their bible...

A Mother's Prayer

Dear Lord,

I don't know what else to do

Don't want to talk too much,

afraid of what it may push her to

I just want her to be safe,

when she's not...

I pray, she finds you in her secret place

That you would be her comfort

and not some cheap escape

I want her to know you,

for herself

I cry out that you take the emptiness

when she feels alone

I pray that you speak louder

than any prayer that I've ever spoke

So she can hear your voice

Be the voice of whom she turns to

Not pulling her down

but lifting her up

My prayers are strong

but as a mother,

I can't keep my tears from wanting to burst

She is my own,

clean or sober

I just want her back

I can pray so many times

Hands and knees grinding the floor

The pain of not knowing,

if she's safe?

Hurts ten times more

So if you hear my prayers Lord,

which I know you do

Keep my daughter safe

Protect her from those who prey

Keep her crown shining, for when she is through

Lord, I thank you,

Amein.

A Mother's Prayer

We as parents face some hard realities when we have children, especially when they are young adults. We can't protect them on consisted bases, like we did when they lived with us and the choices they make are up to them to fix. No matter what they may choose and how much it may hurt us, our hands are often tied. Prayer changes things!

As a mother who saw my child go through complete hell, I know it works. I encourage you to untie your hands, get into your prayer position, and let our Father handle HIS child because after all, we were only assigned to be their physical guardians on this earth. Trust the process and have faith that our Elohim will not fail us or them. Keep in mind; our

children are vessels to be used for His glory as well.

My daughter is sober and herself again. That is

my testimony, I've been there. ~JB~

Beautiful Soul

That Beautiful Soul,
you so gracefully hold
Tranquilizing to a World so cold,
brings joy to the darkest hole
Shine your light, ever so bright
Changing lives in desperate times,
one lost soul at a time

Oh, beautiful soul
Don't ever let your story go untold
Yearning ears need your hope,
they need to know
For it may be the last words,
sliding off your transparent lips
that catches the train of thoughts of some,
who want to flick the switch

Love them, show them, speak life through them
Let them see a living testimony
Give them a bit of faith
A way to escape
Show them the God in you

Be that

Beautiful Soul

that you so gracefully hold

Believe it or not, someone is in need of your light.
Someone needs you to pull through and share your testimony
of how you came out of your storm. Someone is watching you.
Be the beautiful soul that they need to survive. We are
vessels and surely weren't put here just for ourselves. Let
your light shine for others, be the salt we were created to be.

Salt and Light

13 *"You are the salt of the earth. But if the salt loses its saltiness, how can it be made salty again? It is no longer good for anything, except to be thrown out and trampled underfoot.*

14 *"You are the light of the world. A town built on a hill cannot be hidden. 15 Neither do people light a lamp and put it under a bowl. Instead they put it on its stand, and it gives light to everyone in the house. 16 In the same way, let your light shine before others, that they may see your good deeds and glorify your Father in heaven.*

~Matthew 5:13-16~

Quarantine Vent-ish

Let's be the greatest that we can be

Quarantined or not, your purpose does not stop

Pick up the good book, Yah's Word never stops

Seek your shelter in Him

Where fear is not a factor for you

Let go of what you're programmed to

Dig into your heart

Ask God to never part,

to give you strength

to get through this life

Give you the comfort, for what you've lost

Ask to be guided,

open your ears to see

open your eyes to hear

Ask your tongue to slice truth

Ground yourself in His unchanging hands

Take a step back

Watch what our mighty Father,

can do through you

You will be amazed

We are "Made in His image"

to be more than just existing

Fast, so you can hear Him clearly

Follow His Laws and Commands

Grab a hold of His robe and don't let go

Let's be the greatest that we can be

You'll know a poem of quarantine was to come. After all, it's been that way for two years. I've seen lots quote a very popular scripture and I looked it up myself:

Go, my people, enter your rooms
and shut the doors behind you;
hide yourselves for a little while
until his wrath has passed by.
Isaiah 26:20

For myself, I took "hiding myself for a little while," very spiritual and took advantage of being away from the distractions. I hide my nose and eyes in His word. I mean what else was I to do under the circumstances? There was purpose behind it and I'm so glad my spirit man moved to do so. We were told not to trust man in more ways than one through His word (Psalms 118: 8, Psalms 146, Hebrews 12:14). Not saying that we can't trust others in the flesh, but not to put them in front of our belief and faith in our Father. Pray for discernment (1 John 4:1). We have to get back into our Fathers arms, especially now. Use these quarantines or anytime away from the distractions to get closer to our Elohim. Be Blessed!

Yah, My HIStory

I refuse to be blinded about what lies beneath

Was born into this world with no truth to my history

Looked high and I looked low

Seemed everything given, was on repeat

The lies they taught, erasing our roots

Or so they thought

You can twist, scramble, & lead us astray

Taking what only you wanted of our story,

then threw the rest of it away

I knew I was born into greatness, the light...

that they couldn't take

Faced sorrows and brokenness,

at such a young age

Molding me into the Queen, our Father created us to be

What is a Queen without her struggle?

Just another unwilling soul, wondering

New roads were paved, locked doors were opened

Bridges were built, when I couldn't see a way

The Father had me locked down, before I even found myself

Always felt alone in this world, a unique, one of a kind

    type of girl

Was never the average, flawed and flawless

A Jackie of all, Yah, given gifts

Some see my light, then give off an instant diss

Not knowing that I was birth into this

I refuse to be blinded about what lies beneath

God's greatness is weaved into the depths of me

Bringing out the Best of me, Yah, my Father,

    the beginning to my history

Her Testimony

If her testimony could speak,

It will tell you that she...was strong, yet extremely weak

In her mind, her spirit, she was weak

In her flesh and in her sleep

She was...

Lost!

and didn't even know it, completely blindfolded!

Although, her Grandmother often told her to always keep the

faith and put God first, she still did things her way

She was taught to persistently pray in the night and in the

day, especially when things didn't go "her expected" way...

Religiously & traditionally chained

If her testimony could speak,

it will tell you that she leaped into adulthood as a teenage

mom

Pregnant at 16, her first child gave her a brand new song
with a pretty fast beat, things seemed so dark, as if her World
just fell apart and she was trapped, stretched out with one
hand holding on tight, trying to keep her feet at ground level
The other cradling a precious child with no light for her sins.
There was so much more to her, so much more drive within.
Her dreams? Shattered! Military career? Gone! College?
Impossible! Thoughts of a teenage mom...
Her mind had quit, yet she didn't show it

If her testimony could speak,
It would tell you that she had relationships where if he left,
she'd stop breathing. She had given these men so much of her,
she questioned, "Who am I?" She saw THEM, looking into
HER mirror
She was sick in her body with brokenness from loving men
who couldn't handle God's gift.

Who broke promises which broke her, was cheated on and hit.

Lowering her standards for infatuations,

Giving her *unbearable depression snatching her child away*

*gun in her side left her with no answers...*pain. Making her

feel less than a mother, less than a woman.

Not yet, knowing or understanding the jewel she was born

into this life with.

If her testimony could speak,

It would tell you that she's been a single mother for more

than 15 plus years. Working two to three jobs at times,

endless nights of no sleep, lacking knowledge of the resources,

and even if she knew, she had too much pride to ask for a

dollar or two. She cried and sobbed on her room floor when

the kids were sleeping, hushing her weeping.

She needed rest, she needed help, frustrated in her body,

mind, and soul. She needed an escape. She felt unappreciated and abused, her hard work felt like a dead end, three children and two niece's, struggling trying to give them the best, not of everything, just love and knowledge.

If her testimony could speak,
It would tell you that she was trapped in a kill zone
Surrounded by attacks of the enemy, improvised explosive devices called IED's, at the left and right while she drove her truck in the days and nights, Her convoy set as sitting ducks on the road, the crowds of people came in like a dust storm, keeping vigilant of the two suburban's that circled about, for hours it seemed.
Sitting outside of Baghdad while just passing an IED, enemy in the area, roads shut down, she thought, "What do we do now??" Calling home, just to hear her parents ask if that was her...

If her testimony could speak

If her testimony could speak

She would say

She didn't have a relationship with God, and yet, she KEPT

God first, and Her Faith

Where she is weak, He makes her strong

Her mind, renewed and her spirit too

There is no more blindfold, she is found!

She learned how to dance to that fast beat,

let the old World she knew, hit the ground

She let it fall at her feet,

she began to realize she's not of this world anyways

She began to let God kiss her scars, she let Him mend her

brokenness

She was in love and not in lust

She got up off the floor and praised Him for her rest to come

He's all she needs

No person could ever give her that type of rest

He is her protector when things get tough,

even when she was in the Middle East covered in dust

Now if that's not a testimony then I don't know what is!

She would say

She's not religious or a traditional follower, those chains are

broken, she takes joy in serving and she does this using her

heart. She's put her trust and her faith fully in God as the

Word spoke, she began to build a relationship! *Hebrews 11:6*

She would say

Yes, she is that teen mom with a brand new song to sing. She

put God first in everything, found that drive within and

drove, shattering the doubts of never living her dreams of

poetically speaking, right into the recruiting office for the

United States Army, took that same drive and plowed right over those impossible voices, earning her Associates, onto her Bachelors, carrying every step of the way that she can do ALL things possible and didn't doubt it one bit! *Philippians 4:13*

She would say

She did make bad choices in men, Thank God that she now understands that Proverbs 31 isn't just another verse, it's her worth. It's where her rubies were all this time, in the same mirror she saw them in, she is just fine. A beautiful gem she is, a rare find. She walks with her head held so high with God's pride, the light shines even in her hard times. She is so very desirable, She is His, Ruby! *Proverbs 3:15*

She would say

She knows her help comes from someone who will never leave her, she knows that when times get tough and she lays there ready to give up, it's only God that lifts her up. She knows that when the food is low and bills are due, it is him that sends help. She stopped rejecting God's blessings, turned them into testimonies, He began to open the doors she could not see. The hard work was finally paying off, God gives to the weary. *Galatians 6:9*

She would say

She should have died, but God showed, it wasn't her time. Many times her life seemed to flash before her eyes, she lifted her spirits to the sky with her dust covered face and places where her tears streaked, had dried, she watched around looking at others mourning, an automatic reminder of how God protected her and brought them all through. *Psalms 59:1*

She would say

Get up & use your voice in which God gave to you, Share your testimony as she did, let them know the goodness of the Lord and what He's brought you through, never be ashamed of your past because it's all for His glory in the end. Let your testimony be heard, let your testimony speak. *Daniel 4:2*

If her testimony could speak

She would say

Her Testimony...

Looks like, Me

I see the beginning at the end of my

tunnel and it's beautiful!

~Poetic JB~

Made in USA - North Chelmsford, MA
1304626_9781734923261
02.14.2022 1724